D.I.Y. MAKE IT HAPPEN

BAKE SALE

VIRGINIA LOH-HAGAN

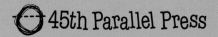

45th Parallel Press

Published in the United States of America by Cherry Lake Publishing
Ann Arbor, Michigan
www.cherrylakepublishing.com

Reading Adviser: Reading Adviser: Marla Conn MS, Ed., Literacy specialist, Read-Ability, Inc.
Book Designer: Felicia Macheske

Photo Credits: © Everything/Shutterstock.com, cover, 1; © Blue Pig/Shutterstock.com, 3, 27; © Lucky Business/Shutterstock.
com, 5; © haveseen/Shutterstock.com, 7; © goodluz/Shutterstock.com, 9; © Pinkcandy/Shutterstock.com, 10, 30; © AS Food
studio/Shutterstock.com, 11; © Nonnakrit/Shutterstock.com, 12, 31; © MJTH/Shutterstock.com, 14; © Winai Tepsuttinun/
Shutterstock.com, 15; © Africa Studio/Shutterstock.com, 15, 26, 30; © arka38/Shutterstock.com, 17; © wavebreakmedia/
Shutterstock.com, 18, back cover; © Kuttelvaserova Stuchelova/Shutterstock.com, 19; © Erika J Mitchell/Shutterstock.com,
20; © Nomad_Soul/Shutterstock.com, 21, back cover; © Monkey Business Images/Shutterstock.com, 23; © RossHelen/
Shutterstock.com, 24; © photka/Shutterstock.com, 25; © Fotos593/Shutterstock.com, 28; © Comaniciu Dan/Shutterstock.
com, 29; © Dora Zett/Shutterstock.com, back cover

Graphic Elements: © IreneArt/Shutterstock.com, 4, 8; © pashabo/Shutterstock.com, 6; © axako/Shutterstock.com, 7; © Katya
Bogina/Shutterstock.com, 11, 19; © Belausava Volha/Shutterstock.com, 12, 24; © Nik Merkulov/Shutterstock.com, 13;
© Sasha Nazim/Shutterstock.com, 15, 22; © Art'nLera/Shutterstock.com, 16, back cover; © Ya Tshey/Shutterstock.com, 16,
17; © kubais/Shutterstock.com, 17; © Elena Nayashkova/Shutterstock.com, 19; © Ursa Major/Shutterstock.com, 20, 28;
© Infomages/Shutterstock.com, 26

45th Parallel Press is an imprint of Cherry Lake Publishing.

Library of Congress Cataloging-in-Publication Data

Names: Loh-Hagan, Virginia, author. I Loh-Hagan, Virginia. D.I.Y. Make it happen.
Title: Bake sale / by Virginia Loh-Hagan.
Description: Ann Arbor : Cherry Lake Publishing, 2016. I Series: D.I.Y. make
   it happen I Includes bibliographical references and index.
Identifiers: LCCN 2016001527I ISBN 9781634711012 (hardcover) I ISBN
   9781634712996 (pbk.) I ISBN 9781634712002 (pdf) I ISBN 9781634713986 (ebook)
Subjects: LCSH: Baking—Juvenile literature. I Baked products—Juvenile
   literature. I Fund raising—Juvenile literature. I Home-based
   businesses—Juvenile literature.
Classification: LCC TX683 .L64 2016 I DDC 664/.752--dc23
LC record available at http://lccn.loc.gov/2016001527

Cherry Lake Publishing would like to acknowledge the work of The Partnership for 21st Century Skills.
Please visit *www.p21.org* for more information.

Printed in the United States of America
Corporate Graphics Inc.

ABOUT THE AUTHOR

Dr. Virginia Loh-Hagan is an author, university professor, former classroom teacher, and
curriculum designer. Her favorite baked good is key lime pie! She lives in San Diego with her
very tall husband and very naughty dogs. To learn more about her, visit www.virginialoh.com.

TABLE OF CONTENTS

CHAPTER ONE

WHAT DOES IT MEAN TO HOST A BAKE SALE?

Do you love cookies? Do you love muffins? Do you love sharing treats? Then hosting a bake sale is the right project for you!

Bake sales are events. People sell **baked goods**. Baked goods are foods that are cooked in an oven. Examples are cakes, pies, and breads.

People host bake sales to earn money. They hold a **fund-raiser**. Fund-raising means making money. People raise money for a **cause**. A cause is a reason. They raise money for a **charity**. A charity helps the community. It's a special group. It does good work. It needs money.

Talk to other people who have hosted bake sales. Get their opinions.

KNOW THE LINGO

Batch cook: making a lot of items that will feed a lot of people

Blind bake: cooking a pie or tart shell before filling it

Budget: the amount of money one has to spend on something

Compote: cooked fruit served in its syrup

Dragées: small, round sugar balls coated with silver and gold that can be eaten and used for decoration

Dust: to lightly coat food with a powdery sugar

Flute: to make a decorative pattern into the raised edge of pie crust dough

Gluten-free: foods that don't have gluten, which is a protein found in wheat, barley, and rye

Icing: a sugary coating frosted on baked goods

Markup: the amount added to the cost of something to determine the selling price

Nonprofit: an organization that does not make more than it spends

Product: goods offered for sale

Pulled sugar: boiled sugar that is used to make flowers and bows for cakes

Revenue: entire amount of profit before costs are taken out

Shortening: solid fat

Host a bake sale whenever you want. They're successful all year long. They're popular events. Schools and churches host bake sales a lot.

Bakers bake food. They follow **recipes**. Recipes are cooking instructions. Bakers work in kitchens. They use ovens. They provide food for bake sales.

Salesmen sell. They take care of money. They serve **customers**. Customers buy things.

You'll have fun hosting your own bake sale. You'll bake yummy treats. You'll sell. You'll meet people. You'll raise money. The best part is tasting the food.

Consider hosting bake sales around holidays and sell holiday treats.

CHAPTER TWO

WHAT DO YOU NEED TO HOST A BAKE SALE?

Decide who gets the **profits**. Profit is money that is earned.

➡ Choose a charity. Or choose a cause.

➡ Consider why the charity needs money.

Create a **committee**. This is a group. It's in charge of the bake sale. Committees plan. They take care of the details.

➡ Assign a **chair**. The chair is the boss.

➡ Assign someone to take care of **publicity**. Make sure people know about the bake sale.

➡ **Assign sales workers. They help customers. They're in charge of money.**

➡ **Assign bakers. Or assign people to get baked goods.**

➡ **Assign helpers. They set up. They also clean up.**

Make a list of everyone's tasks.

Decide the type of bake sale you want to host.

→ **There's a donation sale. Committee members ask for baked goods. People or companies donate food. Donating means giving as a gift. This bake sale has many different kinds of treats.**

→ **There's a volume sale. Volume refers to numbers. The chair chooses two or three food items. The chair tells members what to make. The chair provides recipes. This bake sale has a lot of a few items.**

Consider a **theme**. A theme is a special idea.

➡ Collect baked goods that support the theme.

➡ Create a fun title. An example is "Chocolate Delight."

Keep track of who is making what baked good.

Decide where to host the bake sale. Location is key. Most people host bake sales outdoors.

➡ Choose a place where many people walk by. Examples are by stores and busy downtown areas.

➡ Check with the city. Make sure you're allowed to be there. Get permission.

➡ Have a backup plan. Decide what you'll do if it rains. You can go inside. You can set up a tent.

➡ Decide how you'll work together.

Decide when to host the bake sale.

➡ Choose a time when a lot of people are around. Examples are community events.

➡ Study the weather report. Pick a sunny day.

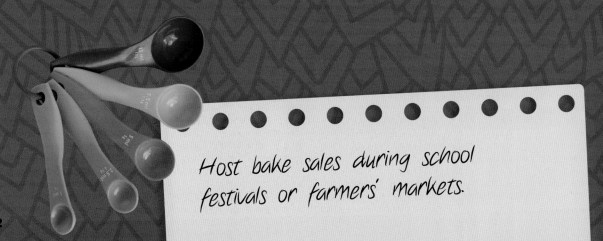

Host bake sales during school festivals or farmers' markets.

TRY THIS!

Create an apple dip station. This can be a small space next to your bake sale. Charge $3 per four apple slices.

You'll need: Granny Smith apples, lemon-lime soda, a large bowl, small bowls, caramel or apple dip, toppings, waxed paper

Steps

1 Cut apples into four pieces. Cut out the seeds.

2 Pour lemon-lime soda into a large bowl.

3 Place slices in this bowl. (This keeps apples from turning brown.)

4 Fill small bowls with caramel dip. (To make apple dip, mix together 8 ounces of cream cheese, ½ cup of brown sugar, and 2 teaspoons of vanilla extract.)

5 Fill small bowls with toppings such as sprinkles, crushed cookies, crushed candy, etc.

6 Give each customer a piece of waxed paper and four apple slices. Have them dip the slices. Then, have them decorate slices with toppings.

Borrow equipment from friends and family.

Besides baked goods, you'll need gear.

➡ **Tables. Use card tables. Use folding tables.**

➡ **Tablecloths. These will cover the tables.**

➡ **Cake stands. These are special dishes that display baked goods.**

➡ **Chairs.**

➡ **Decorations and signs.**

➡ **A cooler. Get ice.**

➡ **Napkins.**

➡ **Small plastic bags or plastic wrap.**

➡ **Shopping bags.**

➡ **A trash can. Get trash bags.**

➡ **A cash box with a lock. It holds money. Include extra money. This is to make change.**

CHAPTER THREE

HOW DO YOU SET UP A BAKE SALE?

Tell people about the bake sale. Make sure people come to the bake sale.

➡ Make flyers. These are signs. Give details about the event. Post flyers at community centers. Post them at local schools. Give flyers to people.

➡ Send e-mails to everyone you know. Send several e-mails. Do this before the event. People need reminders.

➡ Post the event on social media. Use the Internet. Draw attention to the event.

➡ Make signs. Put these where people can see them. Point people to the location of the bake sale.

Advice from the Field
LEIGH SALUZZI

Leigh Saluzzi is a leader of the Atlanta Veg Fest. This festival supports plant-based lifestyles. She's organized many bake sales. She said, "Do it! It doesn't matter how small your sale is." Bake sales are a good way to feed people good food. They're also a good way to raise money. She advises, "People want both sweet and savory options. So don't shy away from baked goods that aren't dessert like cheesy biscuits, mini pizza rounds, mini quiches and the like." Savory foods are more salty. She offers this tip: "Stuff two cookies with frosting for a cookie sandwich! That way you make something extra fun and you can also raise more funds by charging a bit more."

Include location, time, and pictures in your publicity materials.

Have enough baked goods.

➡ **Make the baked goods. D**o this the day before the event. Keep the food fresh. Follow recipes. Keep the baking area clean.

➡ **Collect the baked goods. D**o this as close to the event as possible. Use plastic gloves when handling food.

Include healthy foods. Make a special section for these foods.

➡ Include whole wheat treats.

➡ Include multigrain treats.

➡ Include gluten-free foods. Gluten is in wheat or flour.

➡ Include vegan treats. These treats don't have eggs, milk, or meat.

Wash your hands often when handling food.

Mark items with nuts. Nuts are a common allergen.

Presentation is everything. Make sure items are pretty. Make people want to buy.

➡ **Package** the baked goods. This refers to how items are put together. Wrap items individually. Or wrap two to three items together.

➡ Use plastic bags. Or use plastic wrap. Let people see the baked goods. Tie the bags with ribbon.

➡ Include labels for each package. Let people know the **ingredients**. Ingredients are things used to make food. Some people have **allergies**. Allergies make people sick.

Set prices.

➡ Decide how much each item will cost.

➡ Price things from $1 to $5. Make sure prices cover how much you spent. Make sure you make a profit.

CHAPTER FOUR

HOW DO YOU RUN A BAKE SALE?

You're ready for the bake sale! The chair makes sure the bake sale is successful.

➡ **Assign jobs.**

➡ **Check people's work.**

➡ **Do whatever needs to be done.**

Make sure there's always food on the table.

Set up the **booth**. The booth is the space for the bake sale.

→ Display the baked goods on the tables. Put some food on the table. Keep other food close by. Replace the food as people buy things.

→ Set up a space for the cash box.

→ Set up a donation box. This is a place where people can donate extra money.

→ Hang a big sign. Include prices. Include the cause.

Provide **samples**. Samples are free bits of food. Let people taste the food. This may encourage people to buy it.

➡ Use a special plate. Get a plastic cover. Let people see the food. But keep it covered. Keep the food fresh. If people don't like the samples, they won't buy the food.

➡ Choose a few of your baked goods.

➡ Cut the baked goods into small pieces.

➡ Place toothpicks in each bit.

➡ Give out samples with napkins.

Consider selling drinks.

➡ Sell cold drinks. Sell water and soda.

➡ Sell hot drinks. Sell tea, coffee, or hot cocoa.

Display a sign that reads "Free Samples."

QUICK TIPS

- Make items that can be stored or frozen for a while. Examples are banana-nut bread or peppermint bark.

- Promote your bake sale. Send a sample box of treats along with a flyer to the local radio or TV station.

- Some bake sale hosts don't set prices. They ask for donations instead. This can get people to pay more.

- Cookies and biscuits are simple. They're also cheap to make. Plus, they stack in neat piles.

- Make little paper cones. Pack in popcorn. Pack in candy. Sell these cones for $1 to $2.

- Turn your bake sale into a social event. Play music. Host contests. Host live cooking demonstrations.

- Find a business to match your profits.

Chat with customers. This makes them more interested in buying things.

Be nice to customers.

⇒ Talk to customers. Ask them about their day.

⇒ Thank them for coming to the bake sale.

⇒ Give a free item to customers who buy a lot.

Place items in a shopping bag.

⇒ Consider using recycled grocery bags.

⇒ Put a note in each bag. Include information about the charity. Encourage people to donate more money. Include information about future bake sales.

Consider selling recipe books.

⇒ Collect recipes of all your baked goods. Include the name of the baker.

⇒ Print a small book with these recipes. Include pictures.

⇒ Sell the books for about $5 to $10.

Keep the signs for future bake
sale events.

Prepare for the end of the bake sale.

➡ **Make an announcement.**

➡ **Get rid of the remaining food. Slash your prices. Sell things for cheap.**

➡ **Let customers finish shopping before you pack up.**

End the bake sale.

➡ **Count the money. Give the money to the charity.**

➡ **Pack up. Clean up.**

➡ **Give the leftovers to your helpers. Consider giving leftovers to a shelter for homeless people. Or donate leftovers to a nursing home. Deliver the leftovers right away. Keep the food fresh.**

➡ **Thank everyone. Thank all the bakers. Thank all your helpers.**

THANK YOU

D.I.Y. EXAMPLE!

STEPS	EXAMPLES
Charity or cause	School field trip to Washington, D.C.
Theme	United States flag: We'll feature red, white, and blue treats. We'll play patriotic music. We'll feature the U.S. flag in our publicity and signs.
Title	"Capital Treats"
Type	Combination of a donation sale and volume sale • Ask local bakeries and grocery stores for donations. • Ask members to make a few signature items.
Special signature items	• "Grand Ole Cookies"– star-shaped cookies with red, white, and blue sprinkles • "My Cupcake Tis of Thee"– chocolate cupcakes with red, white, and blue frosting • "Yankee Snickerdoodles"– snickerdoodle cookies frosted with red, white, and blue dots

STEPS	EXAMPLES
Where	At a local farmers' market.
When	Saturday morning
Packaging	◆ 3 cookies per bag ◆ 1 cupcake per bag ◆ 2 bread slices per bag
Fees	◆ $2 per bag ◆ Donation box

GLOSSARY

allergies (AL-ur-jeez) things that make people react and cause sicknesses

baked goods (BAYKD GUDZ) foods that are cooked in an oven

booth (BOOTH) bake sale station or area

cause (KAWZ) a reason to do something

chair (CHAIR) the leader of a committee

charity (CHAR-ih-tee) a group that helps the community and needs money to do it

committee (kuh-MIT-ee) a group of people in charge of something

customers (KUHS-tuh-murz) people who buy things

donation (doh-NAY-shuhn) a gift, such as goods or money, that is given

flyers (FLYE-urz) paper signs

fund-raiser (FUHND-rayz) an event that raises money for a cause

gluten (GLOO-tun) substance in wheat and certain flours

ingredients (in-GREE-dee-uhnts) things used to make food dishes

package (PAK-ij) to present or put together items

profits (PRAH-fits) earned money

publicity (puh-BLIS-ih-tee) the advertising for an event

recipes (RES-uh-peez) instructions to make a food dish

samples (SAM-puhlz) free bits of food used to sell goods

slash (SLASH) cut down prices a lot

theme (THEEM) an idea

vegan (VEE-guhn) foods that don't use any animal products including milk and eggs

volume (VAHL-yoom) number

INDEX

LEARN MORE

BOOKS

Bizainy Charity Bake Sale Activity Kit (Bizainy)

Sennett, Frank. *FUNdraising: 50 Proven Strategies for Successful School Fundraisers*. Thousand Oaks, CA: Corwin, 2008.

Wolf, Laurie Goldrich, and Pam Abrams. *The Only Bake Sale Cookbook You'll Ever Need: 201 Mouthwatering, Kid-Pleasing Treats*. New York: HarperCollins, 2008.

WEB SITES

PTO Today—Bake Sales Step by Step: https://www.ptotoday.com/pto-today-articles/article/664-bake-sales-step-by-step

WikiHow—How to Plan a Bake Sale: www.wikihow.com/Plan-a-Bake-Sale